America and Other Poems

America and Other Poems
J.M. Whitfield

MINT EDITIONS

America and Other Poems was first published in 1853.

This edition published by Mint Editions 2021.

ISBN 9781513282602 | E-ISBN 9781513287621

Published by Mint Editions®

MINT EDITIONS

minteditionbooks.com

Publishing Director: Jennifer Newens
Design & Production: Rachel Lopez Metzger
Project Manager: Micaela Clark
Typesetting: Westchester Publishing Services

To
Martin R. Delany, M.D.

This volume is inscribed as a small tribute of respect,
For his character,
Admiration of his talents, and love of his principles,
By the author

Contents

Introduction

"Another book of poetry," exclaims the reader; "and that, too, by one of the proscribed race, whose lot has been ignorance and servitude." It is even so: and this little volume is presented to the public in the full confidence that it will be read and appreciated, when the circumstances of its origin are known. Its merits as a literary production, we leave to be decided upon by the kind judgment of the American people. We do not claim that the poetry is of the highest order: but we do claim that it would be creditable to authors of greater pretensions than the humble colored man, who hath wrought it out amid the daily and incessant toil necessary for the maintenance of a family, who are dependent upon the labor of his hands for support. There is in it the fire of a genius which, under more favored circumstances, would have soared high, obtained no mean place in the world's estimation. There is the voice of true poesy speaking in it, which, though in the rough it may be, and wanting the polish which education and refined opportunity give, yet nature outgusheth in harmonious numbers, and her bard, all untutored as he is, singeth sweetly, and giveth forth the conceptions of his soul in "words that breathe and thoughts that burn."

The writer of the following pages is a poor colored man of this city, engaged in the humble, yet honorable and useful occupation of a barber. His time is constantly taken up in his business, and he writes in such intervals of leisure as he is able to realize. He is uneducated; not entirely, but substantially; his genius is native and uncultivated, and yet his verse possesses much of the finish of experienced authorship; there is the "ring of the true metal" in it. He feels the "Divine spark" within him, and longs for the means and opportunity to call in the aid of intellectual culture, that he may be enabled to give it form and shape, and clothe it in befitting language. This volume is presented to the public with this view, and in the hope that it may find a favorable reception with our people, and "put money in the purse" of the writer, that he may be able to cultivate, improve, and fully develop the talent which God hath given him.

BUFFALO, MAY, 1853

AMERICA

America, it is to thee,
Thou boasted land of liberty,—
It is to thee I raise my song,
Thou land of blood, and crime, and wrong.
It is to thee, my native land,
From whence has issued many a band
To tear the black man from his soil,
And force him here to delve and toil;
Chained on your blood-bemoistened sod,
Cringing beneath a tyrant's rod,
Stripped of those rights which Nature's God
    Bequeathed to all the human race,
Bound to a petty tyrant's nod,
    Because he wears a paler face.
Was it for this, that freedom's fires
Were kindled by your patriot sires?
Was it for this, they shed their blood,
On hill and plain, on field and flood?
Was it for this, that wealth and life
Were staked upon that desperate strife,
Which drenched this land for seven long years
With blood of men, and women's tears?
When black and white fought side by side,
    Upon the well-contested field,—
Turned back the fierce opposing tide,
    And made the proud invader yield—
When, wounded, side by side they lay,
    And heard with joy the proud hurrah
From their victorious comrades say
    That they had waged successful war,
The thought ne'er entered in their brains
    That they endured those toils and pains,
To forge fresh fetters, heavier chains
For their own children, in whose veins
Should flow that patriotic blood,
So freely shed on field and flood.

Oh no; they fought, as they believed,
    For the inherent rights of man;
But mark, how they have been deceived
    By slavery's accursed plan.
They never thought, when thus they shed
    Their heart's best blood, in freedom's cause
That their own sons would live in dread,
    Under unjust, oppressive laws:
That those who quietly enjoyed
    The rights for which they fought and fell,
Could be the framers of a code,
    That would disgrace the fiends of hell!
Could they have looked, with prophet's ken,
    Down to the present evil time,
    Seen free-born men, uncharged with crime,
Consigned unto a slaver's pen,—
Or thrust into a prison cell,
With thieves and murderers to dwell—
While that same flag whose stripes and stars
Had been their guide through freedom's wars
As proudly waved above the pen
Of dealers in the souls of men!
Or could the shades of all the dead,
    Who fell beneath that starry flag,
Visit the scenes where they once bled,
    On hill and plain, on vale and crag,
By peaceful brook, or ocean's strand,
    By inland lake, or dark green wood,
Where'er the soil of this wide land
    Was moistened by their patriot blood,—
And then survey the country o'er,
    From north to south, from east to west,
And hear the agonizing cry
Ascending up to God on high,
From western wilds to ocean's shore,
    The fervent prayer of the oppressed;
The cry of helpless infancy
    Torn from the parent's fond caress

By some base tool of tyranny,
    And doomed to woe and wretchedness;
The indignant wail of fiery youth,
    Its noble aspirations crushed,
Its generous zeal, its love of truth,
    Trampled by tyrants in the dust;
The aerial piles which fancy reared,
    And hopes too bright to be enjoyed,
Have passed and left his young heart seared,
    And all its dreams of bliss destroyed.
The shriek of virgin purity,
    Doomed to some libertine's embrace,
Should rouse the strongest sympathy
    Of each one of the human race;
And weak old age, oppressed with care,
    As he reviews the scene of strife,
Puts up to God a fervent prayer,
    To close his dark and troubled life.
The cry of fathers, mothers, wives,
    Severed from all their hearts hold dear,
And doomed to spend their wretched lives
    In gloom, and doubt, and hate, and fear;
And manhood, too, with soul of fire,
And arm of strength, and smothered ire,
Stands pondering with brow of gloom,
Upon his dark unhappy doom,
Whether to plunge in battle's strife,
And buy his freedom with his life,
And with stout heart and weapon strong,
Pay back the tyrant wrong for wrong,
Or wait the promised time of God,
    When his Almighty ire shall wake,
And smite the oppressor in his wrath,
And hurl red ruin in his path,
And with the terrors of his rod,
    Cause adamantine hearts to quake.
Here Christian writhes in bondage still,
    Beneath his brother Christian's rod,

And pastors trample down at will,
　　The image of the living God.
While prayers go up in lofty strains,
　　And pealing hymns ascend to heaven,
The captive, toiling in his chains,
　　With tortured limbs and bosom riven,
Raises his fettered hand on high,
　　And in the accents of despair,
To him who rules both earth and sky,
　　Puts up a sad, a fervent prayer,
To free him from the awful blast
　　Of slavery's bitter galling shame—
Although his portion should be cast
　　With demons in eternal flame!
Almighty God! 't is this they call
　　The land of liberty and law;
Part of its sons in baser thrall
　　Than Babylon or Egypt saw—
Worse scenes of rapine, lust and shame,
　　Than Babylonian ever knew,
Are perpetrated in the name
　　Of God, the holy, just, and true;
And darker doom than Egypt felt,
May yet repay this nation's guilt.
Almighty God! thy aid impart,
And fire anew each faltering heart,
And strengthen every patriot's hand,
Who aims to save our native land.
We do not come before thy throne,
　　With carnal weapons drenched in gore,
Although our blood has freely flown,
　　In adding to the tyrant's store.
Father! before thy throne we come,
　　Not in the panoply of war,
With pealing trump, and rolling drum,
　　And cannon booming loud and far;
Striving in blood to wash out blood,
　　Through wrong to seek redress for wrong;

For while thou 'rt holy, just and good,
    The battle is not to the strong;
But in the sacred name of peace,
    Of justice, virtue, love and truth,
We pray, and never mean to cease,
    Till weak old age and fiery youth
In freedom's cause their voices raise,
And burst the bonds of every slave;
Till, north and south, and east and west,
The wrongs we bear shall be redressed.

CHRISTMAS HYMN

Hail, glorious morn! whose radiant beams,
　　Looked down on Christ's nativity,
For every year thy presence teems
　　With joy and glad festivity.

On Judea's plains th' angelic throng
　　Burst on the shepherds' awe-struck gaze,
And raised on high a new-made song
　　Unto their great Creator's praise.

The star of Bethlehem's heavenly light
　　Guided the wise men from the east,
Who came to lay their power and might,
　　Their wisdom, at the Saviour's feet.

Oh, may that star's resplendent light
　　Continue o'er the world to shine,
Till nations now in Pagan night
　　Shall worship at thy holy shrine.

Till all the people of the earth,
　　From north to south, from east to west,
Hear tidings of the Saviour's birth,
　　And bow unto his great behest.

Till superstition's blighting sway
　　Shall flee before religion's light,
As doth the glorious orb of day
　　Disperse the shadows of the night.

Lines on the Death of J. Quincy Adams

The great, the good, the just, the true,
    Has yielded up his latest breath;
The noblest man our country knew,
    Bows to the ghastly monster, Death
The son of one whose deathless name
    Stands first on history's brightest page;
The highest on the list of fame
    As statesman, patriot, and sage.

In early youth he learned to prize
    The freedom which his father won;
The mantle of the patriot sire,
    Descended on his mightier son.
Science, her deepest hidden lore
    Beneath his potent touch revealed;
Philosophy's abundant store,
    Alike his mighty mind could wield.

The brilliant page of poetry
    Received additions from his pen,
Of holy truth and purity,
    And thoughts which rouse the souls of men!
Eloquence did his heart inspire,
    And from his lips in glory blazed,
Till nations caught the glowing fire,
    And senates trembled as they praised!

While all the recreant of the land
    To slavery's idol bowed the knee—
A fawning, sycophantic band,
    Fit tools of petty tyranny—
He stood amid the recreant throng,
    The chosen champion of the free,
And battled fearlessly and long
    For justice, right, and liberty.

What though grim Death has sealed his doom
 Who faithful proved to God and us;
And slavery, o'er the patriot's tomb
 Exulting, pours its deadliest curse;
Among the virtuous and free
 His memory will ever live;
Champion of right and liberty,
 The blessings, truth and virtue give.

To Clinque

All hail! thou truly noble chief,
 Who scorned to live a cowering slave;
Thy name shall stand on history's leaf,
 Amid the mighty and the brave:
Thy name shall shine, a glorious light
 To other brave and fearless men,
Who, like thyself, in freedom's might,
 Shall beard the robber in his den.
Thy name shall stand on history's page,
 And brighter, brighter, brighter glow,
Throughout all time, through every age,
 Till bosoms cease to feel or know
 "Created worth, or human woe."
Thy name shall nerve the patriot's hand
 When, 'mid the battle's deadly strife,
The glittering bayonet and brand
 Are crimsoned with the stream of life:
When the dark clouds of battle roll,
And slaughter reigns without control,
Thy name shall then fresh life impart,
And fire anew each freeman's heart.
Though wealth and power their force combine
 To crush thy noble spirit down,
There is above a power divine
 Shall bear thee up against their frown.

New Year's Hymn

Another year, another year,
    Unfolds its page of hope and fear!
Where, at its close, shall we appear
    Who now are congregated here.

Perhaps, with those now passed away,
    We may be laid deep in the earth;
Perchance, 'mid foreign scenes, we may
    Forget the land that gave us birth.

Perhaps upon the stormy seas,
    Where raging billows wildly roll,
The terrors of despair may seize
    Upon the dark and guilty soil.

But wheresoe'er our footsteps tend,
    'Mid tropic sands, or polar snow,
May we remember that great Friend
    Who guards us wheresoe'er we go.

Whose mighty hand hath been our stay
    Through scenes of trouble, doubt and fear,
And suffered us, poor worms of clay,
    To enter on another year.

To A.H.

I Just had turned the classic page,
     With ancient lore and wisdom fraught,
Which many a hoary-headed sage
     Had stamped with never-dying thought;
And many a bard of lofty mind,
     With measured lay and tuneful lyre,
And strains too grand for human kind,
     All pregnant with celestial fire—
In notes majestic, loud and long,
Had poured the volumed tide of song.
Here Egypt's sages, skilled of yore
     In Isis' dark mysterious rites,
Unvailed their fund of mystic lore
     To eager Grecian neophytes.
And as I sadly musing sat,
     Thinking on ages long gone by,
The Pantheon arose in state,
     And passed before my fancy's eye.
Juno's majestic mien was there,
     And Venus' beauteous form and face,
Diana, modest, chaste, and fair,
     Hebe, adorned with youthful grace,
Ceres, with sheaves and plenteous horn,
     Minerva, with high wisdom crowned,
Aurora, radiant as the morn,
     Whose smiles shed light on all around;
The Graces, sisterhood divine,
     Prepared to charm each mortal sense,
And last of all, the immortal Nine,
     With music, verse, and eloquence,—
Naiads and Nymphs, a numerous train,
Came thronging through the ample fane.
Peris, from eastern regions came,
     Bearing aloft the sacred fire,
Which Zoroaster, son of flame,
     Kindled on Mithra's ancient pyre.

The dark-eyed maids who wait to greet
    The Moslem brave in Paradise,
Forsook awhile their blissful seat,
    And left the region of the skies,
The palm of beauty to dispute
With sovereign Jove's immortal suit.
And as I sat, entranced, amazed,
    With radiant beauty circled round,
They form, high o'er the rest upraised,
    Appeared, with brighter splendor crowned
And every eye was turned on thee,
    Of Houri, Peri, Goddess, Grace,
As, bright in peerless majesty,
    You mounted to the highest place.
Juno resigned her crown to thee,
    Venus her zone of love unbound,
While haughty Pallas bowed the knee,
    And laid her armor on the ground.
The Muses, also, owned thee queen
    Of music, eloquence, and verse,
And tuned their lyres and harps, I ween,
    Thy matchless praises to rehearse.
The Peri owned thy dazzling eye
    Might kindle far a brighter fire
Than that which erst blazed to the sky,
    On many an oriental pyre,
There lighting up with ray divine,
The ancient Gheber's fiery shrine.
The Houris owned that could they charms
    Be viewed from regions of the skies,
'T would tempt the faithful from their arms,
    And all the joys of Paradise;
Or were the Prophet's self on earth,
    And but a glimpse of thee were given,
He'd own one smile of thine were worth
    All pleasures of his highest Heaven;
And from the Moslem creed erase
    That portion so unjustly given,

Which shuts one half the human race
    Forever from the joys of Heaven.
And all the bright Olympic train,
Finding the contest waged in vain,
And that each boasted Deity
Was far eclipsed in charms by thee,
Fled from the scene where all their charms,
    The power of wisdom, beauty, grace,
Had prostrate sunk beneath the arms
    Of one who, though of mortal race,
In her own person did combine
All of the attributes divine
Which Grecian fancy erst did trace
In Nymph, in Goddess, or in Grace;
And ne'er did eastern poet tell,
'Mid all the fabled sprites that dwell
On earth, in water, or in air,
Of aught that could with thee compare—
Of mortal, or immortal kind,
In grace of person and of mind:
For in thy presence pleasures grow,
    And brightest glories round thee move,
Whether it be with men below,
    Or seraphs in the realms above
And when thy spirit shall return
    Back to that Heaven from whence it came,
Angels and seraphs, in their turn,
    Shall join to celebrate thy name,
And spread through Heaven as well as earth,
The story of thy matchless worth.

LOVE

In the bright dreams of early youth,
    I strung my lyre, and waked a strain,
In praise of friendship, love and truth,
    Without a thought of care or pain;
    But soon, in answer to my strain,
A voice came pealing from above;
    Sounding o'er valley, hill and plain—
Where's he that knows the power of love?

The brainless youth in lady's bower,
    Who, sighing, chants some amorous lay,
Or twines a wreath, or plucks a flower,
    A tribute of his love to pay
    Or, mid the crowd, the gallant gay,
With witty jest, and jibe, and jeer,
    Spending in revelry and play
The few bright hours allowed him here,

Thinks that he knows what 't is to love—
    Speaks of that pure and holy flame
Which emanates from God above,
    As though 't were nothing but a name
    That noble, pure, and holy flame,
Jehovah's chiefest attribute,
    Implanted in the human frame,
Raised man above the sordid brute.

And he who ever feels its power,
    Whate'er his station, high or low,
In pleasure's or in sorrow's hour,
    Will feel his inmost bosom glow
    With love to all, both friend and foe;
For God commandeth all to love,
    And those who would his glories know,
Must learn this truth, that God is love.

How Long

How long, oh gracious God! how long
    Shall power lord it over right?
The feeble, trampled by the strong,
    Remain in slavery's gloomy night.
In every region of the earth,
    Oppression rules with iron power,
And every man of sterling worth,
    Whose soul disdains to cringe, or cower
Beneath a haughty tyrant's nod,
And, supplicating, kiss the rod,
That, wielded by oppression's might,
Smites to the earth his dearest right,
The right to speak, and think, and feel,
    And spread his uttered thoughts abroad,
To labor for the common weal,
    Responsible to none but God—
Is threatened with the dungeon's gloom,
The felon's cell, the traitor's doom;
And treacherous politicians league
    With hireling priests, to crush and ban
All who expose their vile intrigue,
    And vindicate the rights of man.
How long shall Afric raise to thee
    Her fettered hand, oh Lord, in vain?
And plead in fearful agony,
    For vengeance for her children slain.
I see the Gambia's swelling flood,
    And Niger's darkly rolling wave,
Bear on their bosoms stained with blood,
    The bound and lacerated slave;
While numerous tribes spread near and far,
Fierce, devastating, barbarous war—
Earth's fairest scenes in ruin laid
To furnish victims for that trade,
Which breeds on earth such deeds of shame
As fiends might blush to hear or name.

I see where Danube's waters roll,
    And where the Magyar vainly strove,
With valiant arm, and faithful soul,
    In battle for the land he loved—
A perjured tyrant's legions tread
The ground where Freedom's heroes bled,
And still the voice of those who feel
Their country's wrongs, with Austrian steel.
I see the "Rugged Russian Bear"
Lead forth his slavish hordes, to War
Upon the right of every State
Its own affairs to regulate:
To help each Despot bind the chain
Upon the people's rights again,
And crush beneath his ponderous paw
All Constitutions, rights and law.
I see in France, oh, burning shame!
The shadow of a mighty name,
Wielding the power her patriot bands
Had boldly wrenched from kingly hands,
With more despotic pride of sway
Than ever monarch dared display.
The Fisher, too, whose world-wide nets
    Are spread to snare the souls of men,
By foreign tyrant's bayonets
    Established on his throne again,
Blesses the swords still reeking red
    With the best blood his country bore,
And prays for blessings on the head
    Of him who wades through Roman gore.
The same unholy sacrifice,
Where'er I turn, bursts on mine eyes,
Of princely pomp, and priestly pride,
    The people trampled in the dust,
Their dearest, holiest rights denied,
    Their hopes destroyed, their spirit crushed;
But when I turn the land to view,
    Which claims, par excellence, to be

the refuge of the brave and true,
 The strongest bulwark of the free,
The grand asylum for the poor
 And trodden-down of every land,
Where they may rest in peace secure,
 Nor fear th' oppressor's iron hand—
Worse scenes of rapine, lust and shame,
Than e'er disgraced the Russian name,
Worse than the Austrian ever saw,
Are sanctioned here as righteous law.
Here might the Austrian's Butcher* make
 Progress in shameful cruelty,
Where women-whippers proudly take
 The meed and praise of chivalry.
Here might the cunning Jesuit learn—
 Though skilled in subtle sophistry,
And trained to persevere in stern,
 Unsympathizing cruelty,
And call that good, which, right or wrong,
Will tend to make his order strong—
He here might learn from those who stand
 High in the gospel ministry,
The very magnates of the land
 In evangelic piety,
That conscience must not only bend
 To every thing the Church decrees,
But it must also condescend,
 When drunken politicians please
To place their own inhuman acts
 Above the "higher law" of God,
And on the hunted victim's tracks
 Cheer the malignant fiends of blood;
To help the man-thief bind the chain
 Upon his Christian brother's limb,
And bear to Slavery's hell again
 The bound and suffering child of Him

---

* Haynau.

Who died upon the cross, to save
Alike, the master and the slave.
While all th' oppressed from every land
Are welcomed here with open hand,
And fulsome praises rend the heaven
For those who have the fetters riven
Of European tyranny,
And bravely struck for liberty;
And while from thirty thousand fanes
    Mock prayers go up, and hymns are sung,
Three millions drag their clanking chains,
    "Unwept, unhonored and unsung;"
Doomed to a state of slavery
    Compared with which the darkest night
Of European tyranny,
    Seems brilliant as the noonday light;
While politicians, void of shame,
    Cry, this is law and liberty,
The clergy lend the awful name
    And sanction of the Deity,
To help sustain the monstrous wrong,
And crush the weak beneath the strong.
Lord! thou hast said, the tyrant's ear
    Shall not be always closed to thee,
But that thou wilt in wrath appear,
    And set the trembling captive free;
And even now dark omens rise
    To those who either see or hear,
And gather o'er the darkening skies
    The threatening signs of fate and fear.
Not like the plagues which Egypt saw,
    When rising in an evil hour,
A rebel 'gainst the "higher law,"
    And glorying in her mighty power—
Saw blasting fire, and blighting hail,
Sweep o'er her rich and fertile vale,
And heard on every rising gale,
Ascend the bitter, mourning wail;
And blighted herd, and blasted plain,

Through all the land the first-born slain,
Her priests and magi made to cower
In witness of a higher power,
And darkness, like a sable pall,
    Shrouding the land in deepest gloom,
Sent sadly through the minds of all
    Forebodings of approaching doom.
What though no real shower of fire
    Spreads o'er this land its withering blight,
Denouncing wide Jehovah's ire
    Like that which palsied Egypt's might;
And though no literal darkness spreads
    Upon the land its sable gloom,
And seems to fling around our heads
    The awful terrors of the tomb:
Yet to the eye of him who reads
    The fate of nations past and gone,
And marks with care the wrongful deeds
    By which their power was overthrown,
Worse plagues than Egypt ever felt
    Are seen wide-spreading through the land,
Announcing that the heinous guilt
    On which the nation proudly stands,
Has risen to Jehovah's throne
    And kindled his avenging ire,
And broad-cast through the land has sown
    The seeds of a devouring fire.
Tainting with foul, pestiferous breath
    The fountain-springs of moral life,
And planting deep the seeds of death,
    And future germs of deadly strife;
And moral darkness spreads its gloom
    Over the land in every part
And buries in a living tomb
    Each generous prompting of the heart.
Vice in its darkest, deadliest stains,
    Here walks with brazen front abroad,
And foul corruption proudly reigns
    Triumphant in the Church of God;

And sinks so low the Christian name,
In foul, degrading vice, and shame,
That Moslem, Heathen, Atheist, Jew,
     And men of every faith and creed,
To their professions far more true,
     More liberal both in word and deed,
May well reject, with loathing scorn,
     The doctrines taught by those who sell
Their brethren in the Saviour born,
     Down into slavery's hateful hell;
And with the price of Christian blood
Build temples to the Christian's God;
And offer up as sacrifice,
     And incense to the God of heaven,
The mourning wail, and bitter cries,
     Of mothers from their children riven;
Of virgin purity profaned
     To sate some brutal ruffian's lust,
Millions of Godlike minds ordained
     To grovel ever in the dust;
Shut out by Christian power and might,
From every ray of Christian light.
How long, oh Lord! shall such vile deeds
     Be acted in thy holy name,
And senseless bigots, o'er their creeds,
     Fill the whole earth with war and flame?
How long shall ruthless tyrants claim
     Thy sanction to their bloody laws,
And throw the mantle of they name,
     Around their foul, unhallowed cause?
How long shall all the people bow
     As vassals of the favored few,
And shame the pride of manhood's brow,
     Give what to God alone is due—
Homage, to wealth, and rank, and power
Vain shadows of a passing hour?
Oh for a pen of living fire,
     A tongue of flame, an arm of steel,

To rouse the people's slumbering ire,
    And teach the tyrant's heart to feel.
Oh Lord! in vengeance now appear,
    And guide the battles for the right,
The spirits of the fainting cheer,
    And nerve the patriot's arm with might;
Till slavery banished from the world,
And tyrants from their powers hurled,
And all mankind from bondage free,
Exult in glorious liberty.

The Arch Apostate

"Since he miscalled the morning star,
Nor man, nor fiend hath fallen so far."

—Bryon

When gathered in the courts above,
    Before Jehovah's burning throne,
Archangels own his boundless love,
    And cast their crowns of glory down;
While cherubim and seraphim,
    Thronging in serried ranks around,
Now raise on high the pealing hymn,
    And loud their Maker's praise resound;
Causing the arch of heaven to ring
With loud hosannas to their king.
And in a thousand varied lays
Pouring their raptured songs of praise,
A tribute to Almighty love,
Through which alone they live and move.
Praising the fixed, unchanging laws,
By which the first Eternal Cause
Propels the radiant spheres on high,
That through the illimitable sky
Pursue their never-varying course
Throughout the boundless Universe.
And all the host to whom was given
    The rays of bright intelligence,
To fit them for the joys of heaven,
    Far higher than the carnal sense;
All owned the wisdom of those laws,
By which the first Almighty Cause,
Throughout Creation's vast expanse,
    Imposed on every creature's mind,
Through endless ages to advance,
    In good and evil unconfined:
That "higher law," which, fixed as fate,

Binds all of high or low estate.
But one, the foremost of that train,
    The first in wisdom, power and might,
Who poured in heaven the highest strain,
    And clearest saw both wrong and right,
Of loftiest, most capacious mind,
    Of largest views, of strongest will,
Of power to dazzle, foil and blind,
    Make evil good, and good seem ill,
With haughty and ambitious boast,
    To deeds of evil e'er inclined,
A third part of the heavenly host
    Drew with him in rebellion blind;
And strove to make a lower law
    Of his own lust, and hate, and pride,
The only source from whence to draw
    For rules and precepts to decide;
And thus beneath his feet he trod
The statues of Almighty God;
And by avenging justice fell
Down to the lowest depths of hell.
So in our Nation's Senate Hall,
    Where statesmen grave, in council meet,
By far the mightiest of them all,
    One called the Godlike, most complete
In all the attributes of mind,
That win the applause of human kind—
Whose learned thoughts, and glowing words,
In early days had oft been poured
In trumpet tones at Freedom's shrine,
And fanned the latent spark divine
Implanted in the human breast,
Of sympathy with the oppressed,
Into a bright and living blaze,
Beneath whose fierce and scorching rays,
Tyrants had cowered in the dust,
And slaves looked up with hopeful trust.
When Greece had broke the tyrant's chain,
    And bathed her sword in Moslem gore,

While Freedom's thrilling battle-strain,
    Was pealing o'er her classic shore,
His was the voice which, o'er the wave,
    Sent forth a loud and cheering note,
Aroused to strife the slumbering slave,
    And cheered the struggling Suliote.
On Plymouth rock his voice was heard,
In tones which like a clarion stirred
The blood in every freeman's veins,
And caused the slaves on Southern plains,
To hail it as the harbinger
    Of bright and halcyon days to come,
When many a Northern Senator
    Shall dare to speak for those now dumb.
But oh, how changed! the giant mind
    That once had soared a Godlike flight,
And, 'mid the sceptered kings of mind
    Had mounted to the loftiest height,
Now prostrate, groveling in the dust,
Recreant to his most sacred trust,
The women-whippers' pliant tool,
    Perjured in sight of God and man,
And falsest of the hollow school
    Of demagogues, who lead the van,
The forlorn hope of slavery;
With intrigue, cunning, knavery,
Striving to quell the rising tide
    Of freedom setting o'er the land,
And threatening with tyrannic pride
    To all who dare for freedom stand,
The terrors of the dungeon's gloom,
The felon's cell, the traitor's doom;
Setting their own unholy laws
    Above the higher law of God
Branding each one who scorns their cause,
    Nor fears the petty tyrant's nod,
A traitor, and an infidel,
And hireling priests are paid to tell
    That those whom Jesus died to save,

And ransomed with his blood from hell,
     Were born to be their abject slaves;
And the rude rabble catch the yell,
And help the furious sound to swell,
Which sends a shout of joy through hell,
Where all the damned, in endless flame,
     Exult amid tormenting fire,
That men should take such pains to claim
     The notice of Almighty ire.
When all the deep-dyed villains come
To listen to their final doom,
And the great Judge himself portrays
     The different degrees of crime
Which marked their darkly devious ways,
     While passing through the rounds of time.
Arnold, whose treacherous nature sought
     His country's freedom to betray,
For which himself had bravely fought,
     On many a doubtful battle-day;
And Gorgey, too, whose jealous spite,
     Betrayed his country to her foes,
And quenched in blood the dawning light
     That brightly o'er her prospects rose;
And Judas, who for paltry pelf,
     His Lord and Saviour basely sold,
And then, despairing, hung himself;
     And all, who, for the lust of gold,
Or pride, or hate, or love of power,
     The tyrant or the traitor played,
Or faltering, in an evil hour,
     Their sacred trusts have all betrayed;
They yet shall scorn the proffered hand
Of him, the vilest of the band,
Who, having greater power of mind
     Than any other living man,
Had used it to debase his kind,
     And spread abroad the direst ban
Which man or devil ever saw,
Slavery's corrupt, inhuman law:

And, sinking from his high estate,
    Without excuse of any kind,
The lust of power, or pride, or hate,
    Or imbecility of mind,
Has stooped in Freedom's council halls,
    Where live the memories of the brave,
To be the meanest thing that crawls
    The earth—a voluntary slave
In future years, when men desire
    To speak in strong hyperbole,
And give, in one small word, the fire
    And essence of iniquity—
That name shall suit their purpose well,
For not 'mid all the fiends of hell,
Could one be found that would express
So well, the depths of littleness;
And Webster's name shall ever be
The deepest badge of infamy.

The Misanthropist

In vain thou bid'st me strike the lyre,
    And sing a song of mirth and glee,
Or, kindling with poetic fire,
    Attempt some higher minstrelsy;
In vain, in vain! for every thought
    That issues from this throbbing brain,
Is from its first conception fraught
    With gloom and darkness, woe and pain.
From earliest youth my path has been
    Cast in life's darkest, deepest shade,
Where no bright ray did intervene,
    Nor e'er a passing sunbeam strayed;
But all was dark and cheerless night,
    Without one ray of hopeful light.
From childhood, then, through many a shock,
    I've battled with the ills of life,
Till, like a rude and rugged rock,
    My heart grew callous in the strife.
When other children passed the hours
    In mirth, and play, and childish glee,
Or gathering the summer flowers
    By gentle brook, or flowery lea,
I sought the wild and rugged glen
    Where Nature, in her sternest mood,
Far from the busy haunts of men,
    Frowned in the darksome solitude.
There have I mused till gloomy night,
    Like the death-angel's brooding wing,
Would shut out every thing from sight,
    And o'er the scene her mantle fling;
And seeking then my lonely bed
    To pass the night in sweet repose,
Around my fevered, burning head,
    Dark visions of the night arose;
And the stern scenes which day had viewed
    In sterner aspect rose before me,

And specters of still sterner mood
    Waved their menacing fingers o'er me.
When the dark storm-fiend soared abroad,
    And swept to earth the waving grain,
On whirlwind through the forest rode,
    And stirred to foam the heaving main,
I loved to mark the lightning's flash,
    And listen to the ocean's roar,
Or hear the pealing thunder's crash,
    And see the mountain torrents pour
Down precipices dark and steep,
    Still bearing, in their headlong course
To meet th' embrace of ocean deep,
    Mementoes of the tempest's force;
For fire and tempest, flood and storm,
    Wakened deep echoes in my soul,
And made the quickening life-blood warm
    With impulse that knew no control;
And the fierce lightning's lurid flash
    Rending the somber clouds asunder,
Followed by the terrific crash
    Which marks the hoarsely rattling thunder,
Seemed like the gleams of lurid light
    Which flashed across my seething brain,
Succeeded by a darker night,
    With wilder horrors in its train.
And I have stood on ocean's shore,
    And viewed its dreary waters roll,
Till the dull music of its roar
    Called forth responses in my soul;
And I have felt that there was traced
    An image of my inmost soul,
In that dark, dreary, boundless waste,
    Whose sluggish waters aimless roll—
Save when aroused by storms' wild force
    It lifts on high its angry wave,
And thousands driven from their course
    Find in its depths a nameless grave.

Whene'er I turned in gentler mood
    To scan the old historic page,
It was not where the wise and good,
    The Bard, the Statesman, or the Sage,
Had drawn in lines of living light,
Lessons of virtue, truth and right;
But that which told of secret league,
    Where deep conspiracies were rife,
And where, through foul and dark intrigue,
    Were sowed the seeds of deadly strife.
Where hostile armies met to seal
    Their country's doom, for woe or weal;
Where the grim-visaged death-fiend drank
    His full supply of human gore,
And poured through every hostile rank
    The tide of battle's awful roar;
For then my spirit seemed to soar
    Away to where such scenes were rife,
And high above the battle's roar
    Sit as spectator of the strife—
And in those scenes of war and woe,
A fierce and fitful pleasure know.
There was a time when I possessed
    High notions of Religion's claim,
Nor deemed its practice, at the best,
    Was but a false and empty name;
But when I saw the graceless deeds
    Which marked its strongest votaries' path,
How senseless bigots, o'er their creeds,
    Blazing with wild fanatic wrath,
Let loose the deadly tide of war,
Spread devastation near and far,
Through scenes of rapine, blood and shame,
Of cities sacked, and towns on flame,
Caused unbelievers' hearts to feel
The arguments of fire and steel
By which they sought t' enforce the word,
    And make rebellious hearts approve

Those arguments of fire and sword
    As mandates of the God of love—
How could I think that such a faith,
    Whose path was marked by fire and blood,
That sowed the seeds of war and death,
    Had issued from a holy God?
There was a time when I did love,
    Such love as those alone can know,
Whose blood like burning lava moves,
    Whose passions like the lightning glow;
And when that ardent, truthful love,
    Was blighted in its opening bloom,
And all around, below, above,
    Seemed like the darkness of the tomb,
'T was then my stern and callous heart,
Riven in its most vital part,
Seemed like some gnarled and knotted oak,
That, shivered by the lightning's stroke,
Stands in the lonely wanderer's path,
A ghastly monument of wrath.
Then how can I attune the lyre
    To strains of love, or joyous glee?
Break forth in patriotic fire,
    Or soar on higher minstrelsy,
To sing the praise of virtue bright,
Condemn the wrong, and laud the right;
When neither vice nor guilt can fling
    A darker shadow o'er my breast,
Nor even Virtue's self can bring,
    Unto my moody spirit, rest.
It may not be, it cannot be!
    Let others strike the sounding string,
And in rich strains of harmony,
    Songs of poetic beauty sing;
But mine must still the portion be,
    However dark and drear the doom,
To live estranged from sympathy,
    Buried in doubt, despair and gloom;

To bare my breast to every blow,
To know no friend, and fear no foe,
Each generous impulse trod to dust,
Each noble aspiration crushed,
Each feeling struck with withering blight,
With no regard for wrong or right,
No fear of hell, no hope of heaven,
Die all unwept and unforgiven,
Content to know and dare the worst
Which mankind's hate, and heaven's curse,
Can heap upon my living head,
Or cast around my memory dead;
And let them on my tombstone trace,
Here lies the Pariah of his race.

A Hymn

*Written for the dedication of the vine street Methodist Episcopal
Church, Buffalo.*

God of our sires! before thy throne
    Our humble offering now we bring;
Deign to accept it as thine own,
    And dwell therein, Almighty King.
Around thy glorious throne above
    Angels and flaming seraphs sing,
Archangels own thy boundless love,
    And cherubim their tribute bring.

And every swiftly rolling sphere,
    That wends its way through boundless space,
Hymns forth, in chorus loud and clear,
    Its mighty Maker's power and grace.
It is not ours to bear the parts
    In that celestial song of praise,
But here, oh Lord! with grateful hearts,
    This earthly fane to thee we raise.

Oh, let thy presence fill this house,
    And from its portals ne'er depart;
Accept, oh Lord! the humble vows
    Poured forth by every contrite heart.
No sacrifice of beast or bird,
    No clouds of incense here shall rise,
But in accordance with thy word,
    We'll bring a holier sacrifice.

Here shall the hoary-headed sire
    Invoke they grace on bended knee,
While youth shall catch the sacred fire,
    And pour its song of praise to thee.
Let childhood, too, with stammering tongue,
    Here lisp thy name with reverent awe,

And high, and low, and old, and young,
    Be brought t' obey thy holy law.

And when our spirits shall return
    Back to the God who gave them birth,
And these frail bodies shall be borne
    To mingle with their kindred earth—
Then, in that house not made with hands,
    New anthems to thy praise we'll sing,
To thee, who burst our slavish bands,
    Our savior, prophet, priest and king.

Yes! Strike Again That Sounding String

Yes! strike again that sounding string,
    And let the wildest numbers roll;
Thy song of fiercest passion sing—
    It breathes responsive to my soul!

A soul, whose gentlest hours were nursed,
    In stern adversity's dark way,
And o'er whose pathway never burst
    One gleam of hope's enlivening ray.

If thou wouldst soothe my burning brain,
    Sing not to me of joy and gladness;
'T will but increase the raging pain,
    And turn the fever into madness.

Sing not to me of landscapes bright,
    Of fragrant flowers and fruitful trees—
Of azure skies and mellow light,
    Or whisperings of the gentle breeze;

But tell me of the tempest roaring
    Across the angry foaming deep,
Or torrents from the mountains pouring
    Down precipices dark and steep.

Sing of the lightning's lurid flash,
    The ocean's roar, the howling storm,
The earthquake's shock, the thunder's crash,
    Where ghastly terrors teeming swarm

Sing of the battle's deadly strife,
    The ruthless march of war and pillage,
the awful waste of human life,
    The plundered town, the burning village!

Of streets with human gore made red,
 Of priests upon the alter slain;
The scenes of rapine, woe and dread,
 That fill the warrior's horrid train.

Thy song may then an echo wake,
 Deep in this soul, long crushed and sad,
The direful impressions shake
 Which threaten now to drive it mad.

To—

Approaching night her mantle flings
    O'er plain and valley, rock and glen,
When borne away on fancy's wings,
    Imagination guides my pen.
I soar away to glittering spheres,
    And leave behind the sons of earth;
Lo! my enraptured fancy hears
    Seraphic strains of heavenly mirth.
A vision as of angel bright
    Sudden appears before my face,
A beauteous, fascinating sprite,
    Endowed with every charm and grace.
Majestic Juno's lofty mien,
    With beauteous Venus' form and face,
And chaste Diana's modesty,
    Adorned with wise Minerva's grace,
United in thy form divine,
With most resplendent luster shine.
And when those matchless charms I viewed,
    Thy faultless form, and graceful mien,
Surprised, amazed, entranced I stood,
    And gazed with rapture on the scene.
And when thy lips were ope'd to speak,
    In tones so sweet, so soft and clear
Gabriel his golden harp might break,
    And seraphs lean from heaven to hear.
'T is the pure mind which dwells within,
    Displays itself in act and word,
And raises thee from every sin
    Far, far above the common herd.
And when the term of life is past,
    And thy pure soul returns to heaven,
The memory of thy worth shall last,
    While thought or mind to man are given

J.M. WHITFIELD

Prayer of the Oppressed

Oh great Jehovah! God of love,
    Thou monarch of the earth and sky,
Canst thou from thy great throne above
    Look down with an unpitying eye?—

See Afric's sons and daughters toil,
    Day after day, year after year,
Upon this blood-bemoistened soil,
    And to their cries turn a deaf ear?

Canst thou the white oppressor bless
    With verdant hills and fruitful plains,
Regardless of the slave's distress,
    Unmindful of the black man's chains.

How long, oh Lord! ere thou wilt speak
    In thy Almighty thundering voice,
To bid the oppressor's fetters break,
    And Ethiopia's sons rejoice.

How long shall Slavery's iron grip,
    And Prejudice's guilty hand,
Send forth, like blood-hounds from the slip,
    Foul persecutions o'er the land?

How long shall puny mortals dare
    To violate thy just decree,
And force their fellow-men to wear
    The galling chain on land and sea?

Hasten, oh Lord! the glorious time
    When everywhere beneath the skies,
From every land and every clime,
    Peans to Liberty shall rise!

When the bright sun of liberty
    Shall shine o'er each despotic land,
And all mankind, from bondage free,
    Adore the wonders of thy hand.

To S.A.T.

As with thy Album in my hand,
    Upon this picture late I gazed,
With tuneful harp held in its hand,
    And eyes of joy to Heaven upraised,
As if it inspiration sought
From Heaven's pure shrine of holy thought,
Like those inspired bards, who sung
Jehovah's praise with prophet tongue,
I thought of thee, as, long ago,
I heard thy voice so sweetly flow
Through measures of most tender feeling,
The soul of melody revealing;
Breathing, in sweetest harmony,
The noblest strains of poesy.
Like seraph of celestial fire,
Who tunes his voice and sacred lyre,
And moves th' angelic hosts above
To pour their notes of praise and love
To Him who sits enthroned on high
In undisputed majesty:
So thy harmonious notes divine
Cause men to bow before *thy* shrine;
Their adoration bring to thee,
Bright image of the Deity.

Delusive Hope

In the bright days of early youth,
    Hope told a fond, delusive tale
Of lasting friendship, holy truth,
    And steadfast love which ne'er should fail.
I listened to the flattering strain
    With all the fire of ardent youth;
And long I sought, but sought in vain,
    To find the dwelling-place of truth.
Though many in her garb appeared,
    Assumed her name and simple mien,
Ere long the vile deceit was cleared,
    And all the hypocrite was seen.
And friendship, too, though long and loud
    Her voice I've heard in many a place,
Among the fickle, thoughtless crowd,
    I never have beheld her face.
Love, next, its bright and glittering chain
    Around the captive fancy threw;
But soon its vows proved false and vain
    As the chameleon's changeful hue.
Now, when the hopes and joys are dead
    That gladdened once the heart of youth,
All the romantic visions fled
    That told of friendship, love and truth,
Turn we unto that steadfast friend
    Who guards our steps where'er they rove,
Whose power supports us to the end,
    Whose word is truth, whose name is love.

To M.E.A.

Oh! had I that poetic lore
    Bestowed upon the favored few,
To ope' Dame Nature's bounteous store,
    And hold her treasures up to view,
To climb Parnassus' lofty mount,
Or taste the Muses' sacred fount,
The far-famed Heliconian spring,
Which Grecian poets erst did sing,—
And did Apollo, and the Nine,
With eloquence and verse divine,
Direct my pen—I scarce could tell
The numerous charms which in thee dwell.
Thy loveliness of form and face
Might serve as model for a Grace;
And the bright luster of thine eye
Mahomet's Houris far outvie.
The nobler beauties of the mind,
    Refined and elevated taste;
Great moral purity, combined
    With every outward charm and grace
And reason, governing the whole,
Displays in every act, a soul
High raised above the things which bind
Down to the earth more sordid minds;
And, soaring fetterless and free
In its unsullied purity,
Seems like a seraph wandering here,
The native of a brighter sphere.

A Hymn

Written for the dedication of the Michigan Street
Baptist Church, Buffalo.

Almighty God! in this thy house,
    For the first time thy people stand,
To pay to thee their humble vows,
    And crave fresh mercies at thy hand.
To thee, oh Lord! this house we rear;
    Deign thou the humble work to bless,
And grant that many souls may hear
    The words of truth and righteousness

Which from thy servants' lips shall fall
    Who labor faithful in thy cause;
Oh may they hear and heed the call,
    And learn t' obey thy holy laws.
Here, often as thy saints shall meet,
    Deign thou to enter in the midst,
And guide our erring, wandering feet,
    In paths which lead to heavenly bliss.

Strengthen the wavering Christian's faith,
    Subdue the proud, exalt the meek,
Save sinners from eternal death,
    And lead us all thy truth to seek.
And when our humble prayers ascend,
    Hear thou, in heaven, thy dwelling-place;
O'er us they guardian arm extend,
    And shed around thy heavenly grace.

And when the pealing hymn shall rise
    In strains of gratitude and praise,
Almighty monarch of the skies,
    Accept and bless our humble lays.
And when thy servants preach thy word,
    Thy Holy Spirit, oh, impart,

And make it like a two-edged sword
    Piercing to every sinner's heart.

And when the toils of life are o'er,
    And these frail bodies turn to dust,
Receive us, Lord, forever more,
    Among the holy and the just.
Then, in that house not made with hands,
    We'll sing new anthems to thy praise,
To thee, who burst our slavish bands,
    And taught our hearts to love they ways.

SELF-RELIANCE

I Love the man whose lofty mind
    On God and its own strength relies;
Who seeks the welfare of his kind,
    And dare be honest though he dies;
Who cares not for the world's applause,
    But, to his own fixed purpose true,
The path which God and nature's laws
    Point out, doth earnestly pursue.
When adverse clouds around him lower,
    And stern oppression bars his way,
When friends desert in trial's hour,
    And hope sheds but a feeble ray;
When all the powers of earth and hell
    Combine to break his spirit down,
And strive, with their terrific yell,
    To crush his soul beneath their frown—
When numerous friends, whose cheerful tone
    In happier hours once cheered him on,
With visions that full brightly shone,
    But now, alas! are dimmed and gone!
When love, which in his bosom burned
    With all the fire of ardent youth,
And which he fondly thought returned
    With equal purity and truth,
Mocking his hopes, falls to the ground,
    Like some false vision of the night,
Its vows a hollow, empty sound,
    Scathing his heart with deadly blight,
Choking that welling spring of love,
Which lifts the soul to God above,
In bonds mysterious to unite
The finite with the infinite;
And draw a blessing from above,
Of infinite on finite love.
When hopes of better, fear of worse,
    Alike are fled, and naught remains

To stimulate him on his course:
    No hope of bliss, no fear of pains
Fiercer than what already rend,
    With tortures keen, his inmost heart,
Without a hope, without a friend,
    With nothing to allay the smart
From blighted love, affection broken,
    From blasted hopes and cankering care,
When every thought, each word that's spoken
    Urges him onward to despair.
When through the opening vista round,
    Shines on him no pellucid ray,
Like beam of early morning found,
    The harbinger of perfect day;
But like the midnight's darkening frown,
    When stormy tempests roar on high,
When pealing thunder shakes the ground,
    And lurid lightning rends the sky!
When clothed in more than midnight gloom,
Like some foul specter from the tomb,
Despair, with stern and fell control,
Sits brooding o'er his inmost soul—
'T is then the faithful mind is proved,
    That, true alike to man and God,
By all the ills of life unmoved,
    Pursues its straight and narrow road.
For such a man the siren song
    Of pleasure hath no lasting charm;
Nor can the mighty and the strong
    His spirit tame with powerful arm.
His pleasure is to wipe the tear
    Of sorrow from the mourner's cheek,
The languid, fainting heart to cheer,
    To succor and protect the weak.
When the bright face of fortune smiles
    Upon his path with cheering ray,
And pleasure, with alluring wiles,
    Flatters, to lead his heart astray,

His soul in conscious virtue strong,
    And armed with innate rectitude,
Loving the right, detesting wrong,
    And seeking the eternal good
Of all alike, the high or low,
His dearest friend, or direst foe,
Seeks out the brave and faithful few,
Who, to themselves and Maker true,
Dare, in the name and fear of God,
To spread the living truth abroad!
Armed with the same sustaining power,
Against adversity's dark hour,
And from the deep deceitful guile
Which lurks in pleasure's hollow smile,
Or from the false and fitful beam
    That marks ambition's meteor fire,
Or from that dark and lurid gleam
    Revealing passion's deadly ire.
His steadfast soul fearing no harm,
    But trusting in the aid of Heaven,
And wielding, with unfaltering arm,
    The utmost power which God has given—
Conscious that the Almighty power
    Will nerve the faithful soul with might,
Whatever storms may round him lower,
    Strikes boldly for the true and right.

Ode for the Fourth of July

Another year has passed away,
And brings again the glorious day
When Freedom from her slumber woke,
And broke the British tyrant's yoke—
Unfurled her standard to the air,
In gorgeous beauty, bright and fair—
Pealed forth the sound of war's alarms,
And called her patriot sons to arms!

They rushed, inspired by Freedom's name,
To fight for liberty and fame;
To meet the mercenary band,
And drive them from their native land.
Almighty God! grant us, we pray,
The self-same spirit on this day,
That, through the storm of battle, then
Did actuate those patriot men!

May those great truths which they maintained
Through years of deadly strife and toil,
Be by their children well sustained,
Till slavery ceases on our soil—
Till every wrong shall be redressed,
And every bondman be set free;
And from the north, south, east and west,
Peans shall rise to Liberty.

May that same God whose aegis led
Our patriot sires on Bunker's height,
Shed the same blessings on our head,
The heroes of a nobler fight—
A fight not waged by fire and sword,
And quenched in gore and human blood,
But only by that Sacred Word,
The mandate of Almighty God.

Our cause is Love, our weapon Truth,
Our ally is the living God;
Matron and maiden, sire and youth,
Shall feel the power of his rod.
Prone to the dust, shall Slavery fall,
And all its withering influence die,
While liberty, the boon of all,
Shall swell through earth, and air, and sky.

Midnight Musings

The gloomy night has cast a shroud
    Upon the dwelling-place of men;
Hushed are the voices of the crowd,
    And silence reigns o'er hill and glen.
My winged fancy takes its flight
    Through the unfathomed dark abyss,
And rends the vail of somber night
    From many scenes of woe and bliss.
I enter first the poor man's cot;
    The sick wife, on her straw-made bed,
Reflects upon her lowly lot,
    While piercing pains distract her head;
The famished children's cries for bread
    Are issued in such piteous tones,
The father hangs his drooping head,
    To hear his wife and children's moans.
The eyes of all that meager train
    Turned upon him to seek relief:
The thought o'erwhelms his burning brain
    With silent but expressive grief.
Near to the cot, a mansion proud
    Raises its stately roof tow'rd heaven;
While mirth and revelry full loud
    Burst on the stillness of the even.
Here wealth spreads her luxurious board,
    And glittering crowds the feast partake,
Not caring how the starving horde
    Of hungry poor their fast may break.
The wealth profusely squandered here,
    In gorgeous dress and proud array,
Would furnish forth good homely cheer
    On many a dreary winter's day,
To those who now, by want oppressed,
    Or smitten by some dire disease,
Pray fervently to God for rest,
    That death may come their pangs to ease.

And do you think a righteous God
    Will listen to your wretched pleas,
That when you saw his chastening rod
    Inflicting famine and disease
Upon your fellow-men, that ye
    Should grant no aid to their distress,
But use your every energy
    To wrong, and crush them, and oppress?
No! when you stand before his bar,
    You'll hear pronounced this awful doom:
"Depart from me, ye cursed, afar,
    And give my humble followers room!"

ODE TO MUSIC

There's music wheresoe'er we roam—
'T is heard in ocean's crested foam,
And in the billows' deafening roar,
Which madly burst upon the shore:
They sing of Heaven's eternal Lord,
Who calms their raging by his word.

There's music in the gentle breeze,
which softly blows among the trees,
Shaking fresh fragrance from the flowers,
In blooming fields and shady bowers;
They sing of Him whose power below,
Caused trees, and grass, and flowers to grow

There's music in the numerous herds,
    Scattered about o'er hills and plains,
And in the flocks of feathered birds,
    Who, in a thousand varied strains,
Praise Him whose all-creating word
Brought into being beast and bird.

There's music in the tempest's sound,
    That darkly sweeps across the wave,
And hangs its shadowy pall around
    The ship-wrecked sailor's ocean grave;
Where the wild waste of waters yell,
Through caverns deep and dark as hell!

It speaks of His almighty power,
    Whose arm is ever stretched to save,
Who, in death's dark and trying hour,
    Can shed a halo round the grave;
And make the ocean's yawning cavern,
A glorious entrance into Heaven.

There's music in the thunder's roar,
    Which peals along the vault of heaven,
While torrents from the mountains pour,
    And trees by the dread bolt are riven;
Seen by the fiery element,
The earth, and sky, and sea seem blent.

It tells of Him whose wondrous power
    Can make the lightning do his will,
And sends the cool refreshing shower
    Upon the just and unjust still;
And whispers in a still, small voice,
To all the sons of earth, rejoice!

But leave this scene of doubts and fears,
    And swift on fancy's pinions fly,
And hear the music of the spheres
    Resounding sweetly through the sky;
They sing of Him, th' incarnate Word
Man's Saviour, Heaven's Almighty Lord!

Where'er we turn, music is found,
    With all its Heaven-born power to charm,
To lull us with its soothing sound,
    And shed around a holy balm—
Pure as the thrilling, heavenly strains
From angels' harps, on Judah's plains.

Shall man, rescued from death and hell,
    Shall he alone refuse to raise
His feeble voice, the song to swell
    Unto his great Creator's praise?
While seraphs and archangels join
The blissful harmony divine.

Then let our tongues fresh music make,
    And sound his wondrous praise abroad;

And when the Universe shall quake,
    And Nature quail before her God,
We'll join the angels' choir above,
And sing our Lord's unchanging love.

Stanzas for the First of August

From bright West Indies' sunny seas,
    Comes, borne upon the balmy breeze,
The joyous shout, the gladsome tone,
    Long in those bloody isles unknown;
Bearing across the heaving wave
The song of the unfettered slave.

No charging squadrons shook the ground,
    When freedom here her claims obtained;
No cannon, with tremendous sound,
    The noble patriot's cause maintained:
No furious battle-charger neighed,
No brother fell by brother's blade.

None of those desperate scenes of strife,
    Which mark the warrior's proud career,
The awful waste of human life,
    Have ever been enacted here;
But truth and justice spoke from heaven,
And slavery's galling chain was riven.

'T was moral force which broke the chain,
    That bound eight hundred thousand men;
And when we see it snapped in twain,
    Shall we not join in praises then?—
And prayers unto Almighty God,
Who smote to earth the tyrant's rod?

And from those islands of the sea,
    The scenes of blood and crime and wrong,
The glorious anthem of the free,
    Now swells in mighty chorus strong;
Telling th' oppressed, where'er they roam,
Those islands now are freedom's home.

THE NORTH STAR*

Star of the north! whose steadfast ray
    Pierces the sable pall of night,
Forever pointing out the way
    That leads to freedom's hallowed light:
The fugitive lifts up his eye
To where thy rays illume the sky.

That steady, calm, unchanging light,
    Through dreary wilds and trackless dells,
Directs his weary steps aright
    To the bright land where freedom dwells;
And spreads, with sympathizing breast,
Her aegis over the oppressed.

Though other stars may round thee burn,
    With larger disk and brighter ray,
And fiery comets round thee turn,
    While millions mark their blazing way;
And the pale moon and planets bright
Reflect on us their silvery light.

Not like that moon, now dark, now bright,
    In phase and place forever changing;
Or planets with reflected light,
    Or comets through the heavens ranging;
They all seem varying to our view,
While thou art ever fixed and true.

So may that other bright North Star,
    Beaming with truth and freedom's light,
Pierce with its cheering ray afar,
    The shades of slavery's gloomy night;
And may it never cease to be
The guard of truth and liberty.

---

* *Written for the North Star; a newspaper edited by a fugitive slave.*

A Note About the Author

J.M. Whitfield (1822–1871) was an African American poet and abolitionist. Born in New Hampshire to Joseph Whitfield, who escaped slavery in Virginia, and Nancy, the daughter of a freed slave, Whitfield was educated in Exeter until his father's death. Having lost his mother at the age of seven, Whitfield was orphaned at just nine years old. Nothing is known about his life until 1839, when records show him as the owner of a barber shop and a home in Buffalo, New York. In his free time, Whitfield published his own writing, and in 1853 found publication with James S. Leavitt of Buffalo for a small volume of poems. America and Other Poems—dedicated to his friend Martin Delany—earned him a reputation as a leading Black poet of his time. His poems on abolition, American history, nature, and political figures appeared in William Lloyd Garrison's The Liberator and Frederick Douglass' The North Star. Alongside Delany, Whitfield became a fierce advocate for the Colonization Movement, marking a major break from the abolitionist faction represented by Douglass. In the early 1860s, Whitfield moved to San Francisco, where he opened another barber shop and joined the Prince Hall Freemasons. He was the grand uncle of Pauline Elizabeth Hopkins, a pioneering novelist and playwright.

A Note from the Publisher

Spanning many genres, from non-fiction essays to literature classics to children's books and lyric poetry, Mint Edition books showcase the master works of our time in a modern new package. The text is freshly typeset, is clean and easy to read, and features a new note about the author in each volume. Many books also include exclusive new introductory material. Every book boasts a striking new cover, which makes it as appropriate for collecting as it is for gift giving. Mint Edition books are only printed when a reader orders them, so natural resources are not wasted. We're proud that our books are never manufactured in excess and exist only in the exact quantity they need to be read and enjoyed.

bookfinity™

Discover more of your favorite classics with Bookfinity™.

- Track your reading with custom book lists.
- Get great book recommendations for your personalized Reader Type.
- Add reviews for your favorite books.
- AND MUCH MORE!

Visit **bookfinity.com** and take the fun Reader Type quiz to get started.

Enjoy our classic and modern companion pairings!

Classic & Modern